The Story of Stones

A Biblical Workbook-Journal for Finding Joy

in the Face of Adversity

By L.J. Nance

Dedication

To Diane Langworthy, who took a leap of faith and let me preach.

The Story of Stones
By L. J. Nance

PRINT:
ISBN - 9798523573255

© Copyright Lara Nance 2021, All rights reserved.
Cover art: Lara Nance

Books/E-books are not transferable. They cannot be sold, shared or given away as it is an infringement on the copyright of this work.

All rights reserved. No part of this book may be used or reproduced in any manner whatsoever without written permission, except in the case of brief quotations embodied in critical articles and reviews.

Consider it pure joy, my brothers and sisters, whenever you face trials of many kinds, because you know that the testing of your faith produces perseverance.
Let perseverance finish its work so that you may be mature and complete, not lacking anything. — James 1:2-4

The purpose of this workbook/journal is to help you transform how you internalize hardships and doubts in life into a more meaningful process, which will lead to greater joy. The Story of Stones is the means of guiding you within this transformation. As you progress through your journey, wisdom widens and understanding blossoms so that you abide in the love of God and know He is always there, patiently and tenderly waiting.

Know that this development may take years, so don't be discouraged if you can't complete every step at the present time. Just keep the story in the back of your mind, and with faith you will be able to view events more clearly as you continue to tumble along in the River of Life.

Most importantly, stay in the river.

Let the Journey begin.

Begin the Journey of your Stone Story. Describe yourself as a rock, sharp edges? Deep crevices? Uneven surfaces filled with shadows? Note why you describe yourself this way. Cut out a picture of a rock that best fits your description and tape it to this page.

_____
_____
_____
_____
_____
_____
_____
_____
_____
_____
_____
_____
_____
_____
_____
_____
_____
_____

"We are all rough drafts of the people we're becoming." – Bob Goff

What sharp edges or rough spots need to be removed and smoothed?
Recognizing our faults as opportunities is the first step to transformation.

_____
_____
_____
_____
_____
_____
_____
_____
_____
_____
_____
_____
_____
_____
_____
_____
_____
_____
_____
_____

I acknowledged my sin to you, and I did not cover my iniquity; I said, "I will confess my transgressions to the Lord," and you forgave the iniquity of my sin. - Psalm 32:5

Uncovering the source of our behavior is vital for change to occur.

What past events, people, or elements of your environment incite you to sin? Does how you were raised affect your behavior in a bad way? What beliefs do you need to change from the past?

___

"I am good, but not an angel. I do sin, but I am not the devil. I'm just a small girl in a big world trying to find someone to love." – Marilyn Monroe

Recognize your beginning, how has it shaped your life?

In the beginning, rocks have uneven surfaces and sharp edges. You can find stones like this anywhere, and they come in all shapes and sizes. They can be on top of the ground, some you have to dig for, and some are so large you can't move them.

_____
_____
_____
_____
_____
_____
_____
_____
_____
_____
_____
_____
_____
_____
_____
_____
_____
_____
_____

"We are all ghosts of yesterday, and the phantom of tomorrow awaits us alike in sunshine or in shadow, dimly perceived at times, never entirely lost."
- Daphne du Maurier

Examine your rough edges in detail, what caused them? Go deep.

_____
_____
_____
_____
_____
_____
_____
_____
_____
_____
_____
_____
_____
_____
_____
_____
_____
_____
_____
_____
_____
_____

"Let us fall before the majesty of our great God, acknowledging our faults, and praying that he will make us ever more conscious of them."
- John Calvin.

Looking at your past, what are events that caused you pain or despair? Why were these events difficult for you?

_____
_____
_____
_____
_____
_____
_____
_____
_____
_____
_____
_____
_____
_____
_____
_____
_____
_____
_____
_____

"The ultimate measure of a man is not where he stands in moments of comfort and convenience, but where he stands at times of challenge and controversy." – Martin Luther King, Jr.

How did these events change you? Look deeper. Are there changes you haven't yet recognized? How did the events help you gain wisdom or change your behavior for the better?

_____
_____
_____
_____
_____
_____
_____
_____
_____
_____
_____
_____
_____
_____
_____
_____
_____
_____
_____
_____

"All the adversity I've had in my life, all my troubles and obstacles, have strengthened me. You may not realize it when it happens, but a kick in the teeth may be the best thing in the world for you." — Walt Disney

How did these adverse events make you stronger? If you've never considered this before, take time to explore and be honest about lessons learned.

_____
_____
_____
_____
_____
_____
_____
_____
_____
_____
_____
_____
_____
_____
_____
_____
_____
_____
_____
_____
_____
_____
_____
_____

"Now, every time I witness a strong person, I want to know: What darkness did you conquer in your story? Mountains do not rise without earthquakes." - Katherine MacKennett

Was there a time you felt completely hopeless, perhaps even considered ending your life? What put you in this position? Was it a hopeless situation or was depression/mental illness a factor?

_____
_____
_____
_____
_____
_____
_____
_____
_____
_____
_____
_____
_____
_____
_____
_____

"Depression is the most unpleasant thing I have ever experienced. It is that absence of being able to envisage that you will ever be cheerful again. The absence of hope. That very deadened feeling, which is so very different from feeling sad. Sad hurts but it's a healthy feeling. It is a necessary thing to feel. Depression is very different." - J. K. Rowling

How did you overcome this hopelessness? List people who helped you, or any other forms of support such as prayer, counseling, or medication. Acknowledge gratitude for the helpers. Was there a sighting of the Holy Spirit in your ability to overcome the hopelessness?

_____
_____
_____
_____
_____
_____
_____
_____
_____
_____
_____
_____
_____
_____
_____
_____
_____
_____

May the God of hope fill you with all joy and peace as you trust in him, so that you may overflow with hope by the power of the Holy Spirit.
– Romans 15:13

Think of yourself as a stone in a river - the River of Life. In a river, a stone can become rounded and smooth, all the rough edges worn away, especially a river filled with rapids that mirror the tumultuous events in our lives. Find a picture of a smooth river stone and tape it to this page. What description comes to your mind when you look at this stone? How long do you think it took for the stone to become smooth?

_____
_____
_____
_____
_____
_____
_____
_____
_____
_____
_____
_____
_____
_____
_____
_____

"We change our behavior when the pain of staying the same becomes greater than the pain of changing." - Henry Cloud

It takes a long time for us as rough rocks to become smooth. Much depends on the sort of stone we are in the beginning. We might be hard or soft, we could be large or small, and some of us have many more protruding sharp edges than others. Our process of smoothing will also depend on the quantity of water in the river as well as how fast it flows and the obstacles in its path. There's also the nature of any abrasive sediment around the stone and probably many other variables. Consider all these variables as the events we endure in our lives.

For instance, going through rapids might be like going through a divorce, and a big boulder in the middle that we crash into might be like losing a job, the abrasive sand we grate against might be a boss we had that treated us badly.

In any event, we're talking years instead of days for this transformation to occur. Some of us are going to need a whole lot of tumbling and a long time to wear down all our rough edges. It takes years for us to learn lessons that perfect us. How many jobs did you have to lose before you stopped worrying about money and believed it when God said He would take care of you? You maybe had to crash into that boulder many times before that rough edge fell away.

Can you think of events in your life that were similar to each other, like marrying more than one abusive spouse, or returning to addiction over and over? Did you learn a lesson from these repeated events? Make a list and describe why you needed more than one event to learn a lesson. How did you finally break the chain of repeated mistakes? If you haven't, how can you?

Make a list of people in your life who were toxic for you. What made them toxic? How did you deal with them? What lessons did they teach you that helped remove a jagged edge from your stone? Find gratitude for the lessons and forgive, let any hatred or bitterness go. If you still identify toxic people in your life, how can you change those relationships, return to peace and lose a jagged edge?

_____
_____
_____
_____
_____
_____
_____
_____
_____
_____
_____
_____
_____
_____
_____
_____

Beloved, never avenge yourselves, but leave it to the wrath of God, for it is written, "Vengeance is mine, I will repay, says the Lord." – Romans 12:19

Now, think of people who had a positive impact on you, mentors, teachers, relatives, or friends. Make a list, describe how they helped you. How did their support remove a jagged edge from your stone?

_____
_____
_____
_____
_____
_____
_____
_____
_____
_____
_____
_____
_____
_____
_____
_____
_____
_____

"None of us got to where we are alone. Whether the assistance we received was obvious or subtle, acknowledging someone's help is a big part of understanding the importance of saying thank you." – Harvey Mackay

From the list on the previous page, send a card or note to each person and thank them, or if they are no longer around, send them a special prayer. Let them know how they helped you and what a difference it made in your life. Practice Gratitude.

_____
_____
_____
_____
_____
_____
_____
_____
_____
_____
_____
_____
_____
_____
_____
_____

"Make it a habit to tell people thank you. To express your appreciation, sincerely and without the expectation of anything in return. Truly appreciate those around you, and you'll soon find many others around you. Truly appreciate life, and you'll find that you have more of it." – Ralph Marston

Have you paid it forward? How have you repaid the help **you** received, by helping others? Make a list of how you have paid it forward and how this helped remove a jagged edge from your surface. Also, list ways you can pay it forward if you haven't.

_____
_____
_____
_____
_____
_____
_____
_____
_____
_____
_____
_____
_____
_____
_____
_____
_____
_____
_____
_____

Do not neglect to do good and to share what you have, for such sacrifices are pleasing to God. - Hebrews 13:16

Our body is the temple of the Holy Spirit. Have you removed any jagged edges that might damage your body? Bear your soul on this page about addictions, untreated illnesses, unresolved stressors, etc. that are causing damage to your body or mind. Resolve to address these issues and repair the Holy Spirit's temple to remove those sharp edges.

_____
_____
_____
_____
_____
_____
_____
_____
_____
_____
_____
_____
_____
_____
_____
_____
_____
_____
_____

Or do you not know that your body is a temple of the Holy Spirit within you, whom you have from God? You are not your own, for you were bought with a price. So, glorify God in your body. – 1 Corinthians 6: 19-20

Stay in the river.

Some rocks lack faith and can't withstand the turbulence of the river. They are tossed out to the side ground where they remain in their rough, unaltered and joyless state. But with faith, we know God is with us and we withstand the tumult of adverse events, learn from them, and proceed to our smooth stone transformation. Are you still in the river? Why or why not?

_____
_____
_____
_____
_____
_____
_____
_____
_____
_____
_____
_____
_____
_____
_____
_____
_____

For you have need of endurance, so that when you have done the will of God you may receive what is promised. - Hebrews 10:36

What has helped you stay in the river? If you left the river, are you able to tumble back in and continue your journey? What would it take to renew your faith?

_____
_____
_____
_____
_____
_____
_____
_____
_____
_____
_____
_____
_____
_____
_____
_____
_____
_____
_____
_____

Create in me a clean heart, O God, and renew a right spirit within me.

- Psalm 51:10

The next chapter in your stone story.

We've tumbled and learned hard lessons from difficult events or tragedies in our life. Due to this, we've let go of things like hatred, racism, or greed, and just like a rough rock, when we let go of those things, it's like the water rushed over and smoothed away a rough edge. We've also learned to pause in our judgements of others, or found that giving back is greater than receiving. The water rushes over us and smooths more rough edges away. We study and learn about God and how to be more like Jesus. The water rushes over us and smooths more rough edges away.

We've arrived at the state where we're rounded and smooth, like a polished pebble in a riverbed. We might think we've made it and there is nothing left to learn, no more rough edges to wash away. We're perfectly smooth, right?

But there is one last stage we need to go through in our transformation. We need to hone our faith, like a laser against a hard stone, and sometimes this can be the most difficult challenge we face in life. Why? Because many times this requires us to go against our nature, the most ingrained part of our soul. Are you ready?

_____

_____

_____

"At any given moment we have two options: to step forward into growth or step back into safety." - Abraham Maslow

How hard is it to go against your nature? It's very, very hard. We might naturally have the urge to fight back when someone hits or hurts us. Our instinct may be to make sharp replies when we become frustrated with someone. We might feel the need to accumulate a lot of money so we can have the things that make life fun and easy. It's also our human nature to fear death or crave love. The list goes on and on.

Name one thing that is part of your nature that you recognize you must go against. Explore how this became part of your nature. Environment, learned from parents, societal pressure?

_____
_____
_____
_____
_____
_____
_____
_____
_____
_____
_____
_____
_____
_____

"There is a great deal of human nature in people." - Mark Twain

What path can you take to reverse engineer this trait and transform to a new nature that reflects God? Who and/or what can assist you in this part of your journey? Make a plan.

_____
_____
_____
_____
_____
_____
_____
_____
_____
_____
_____
_____
_____
_____
_____
_____
_____
_____
_____
_____

"There is nothing that can be changed more completely than human nature when the job is taken in hand early enough." - George Bernard Shaw

Work your plan. This element of your nature didn't occur overnight. It won't be easy to change, nor will that change take place overnight. How can you sustain yourself during this time of difficult transition? Like a swift flowing river full of boulders in your path and rapids to navigate, what obstacles stand in your way? List them and then, one by one, eliminate them. List the sustaining forces that will aid you.

_____
_____
_____
_____
_____
_____
_____
_____
_____
_____
_____
_____
_____
_____
_____
_____
_____

"Nothing is so painful to the human mind as great and sudden change."
- Mary Wollstonecraft Shelley

What is your goal? Have you misidentified your goal? As earthly beings, we grow up thinking life is all about going to school, getting a job, making money to buy a nice house and car, maybe finding a spouse and having a family, and then retiring to travel for fun.

That's not what life is about for Christians. God's great plan is to defeat evil once and for all and everything here is leading up to that, so that He can gather us home and have peace at last. We are fighting alongside Him, and things that happen along our path are there to strengthen us, educate us and prepare us to join Him in Heaven. Making Heaven our goal is one of the most important parts of this last stage. Is Heaven your goal? Why or why not?

_____
_____
_____
_____
_____
_____
_____
_____
_____
_____
_____
_____

"The Lord looks down from Heaven on the children of man, to see if there are any who understand, who seek after God." - Psalm 14:2

It's important to dwell on the concept of Heaven as a goal.

It's also important to dispel the fictional notion that Heaven is some cloudy, boring place where we'll float around playing harps all day. Read these passages from the Bible about Heaven and visualize its beauty and majesty. Feel the joy of making this place your goal.

HEAVEN

"On this mountain, the Lord of hosts will make for all peoples a feast of rich food, a feast of well-aged wine, of rich food full of marrow, of aged wine well refined. And He will swallow up on this mountain the covering that is cast over all peoples, the veil that is spread over all nations. He will swallow up death forever; and the Lord God will wipe away tears from all faces, and the reproach of His people He will take away from all the earth, for the Lord has spoken. It will be said on that day, "Behold, this is our God; we have waited for Him, that He might save us. This is the lord; we have waited for Him; let us be glad and rejoice in His salvation."
– Isaiah 25:6-9

Therefore, they are before the throne of God, and serve Him day and night in His temple; and He who sits on the throne will shelter them with his presence. They shall hunger no more, neither thirst anymore; the sun shall not strike them, nor any scorching heat. For the Lamb in the midst of the throne will be their shepherd, and he will guide them to springs of living water, and God will wipe away every tear from their eyes."
- Revelation 7:15-17

Let not your hearts be troubled. Believe in God; believe also in me. In my Father's house are many mansions. If it were not so, would I have told you that I go to prepare a place for you?
- John 14:1-2

For we know that if the tent that is our earthly home is destroyed, we have a building from God, a house not made with hands, eternal in the heavens. For in this tent we groan, longing to put on our heavenly dwelling, if indeed by putting it on we may not be found naked. For while we are still in this tent, we groan, being burdened- not that we would be unclothed, but that we would be further clothed, so that what is mortal may be swallowed up by life. He who has prepared us for this very thing is God, who has given us the Spirit as a guarantee.
- 2 Corinthians 5:1-5

Then the angel showed me the river of the water of life, bright as crystal, flowing from the throne of God and of the Lamb through the middle of the street of the city; also, on either side of the river, the tree of life with its twelve kinds of fruit, yielding its fruit each month. The leaves of the tree were for the healing of the nations. No longer will there be anything accursed, but the throne of God and of the Lamb will be in it, and his servants will worship him. They will see his face, and his name will be on their foreheads. And night will be no more. They will need no light of lamp or sun, for the Lord God will be their light, and they will reign forever and ever.
- Revelation 22:1-5

But, as it is written, "What no eye has seen, nor ear heard, nor the heart of man imagined, what God has prepared for those who love him
- 1 Corinthians 2:9

And the twelve gates were twelve pearls, each of the gates made of a single pearl, and the street of the city was pure gold, transparent as glass. And I saw no temple in the city, for its temple is the Lord God the Almighty and the Lamb. And the city has no need of sun or moon to shine on it, for the glory of God gives it light, and its lamp is the Lamb. By its light will the nations walk, and the kings of the earth will bring their glory into it, and its gates will never be shut by day—and there will be no night there.
- Revelation 21:21-25

But according to his promise we are waiting for new heavens and a new earth in which righteousness dwells.
- 2 Peter 3:13

But you have come to Mount Zion and to the city of the living God, the heavenly Jerusalem, and to innumerable angels in festal gathering, and to the assembly of the firstborn who are enrolled in heaven, and to God, the judge of all, and to the spirits of the righteous made perfect, and to Jesus, the mediator of a new covenant, and to the sprinkled blood that speaks a better word than the blood of Abel.
- Hebrews 12:22-24

Then I saw a new heaven and a new earth, for the first heaven and the first earth had passed away, and the sea was no more. And I saw the holy city, new Jerusalem, coming down out of heaven from God, prepared as a bride

adorned for her husband. And I heard a loud voice from the throne saying, "Behold, the dwelling place of God is with man. He will dwell with them, and they will be his people, and God himself will be with them as their God. He will wipe away every tear from their eyes, and death shall be no more, neither shall there be mourning, nor crying, nor pain anymore, for the former things have passed away." And he who was seated on the throne said, "Behold, I am making all things new." Also, he said, "Write this down, for these words are trustworthy and true.
- Revelation 21:1-27

The wolf will live with the lamb, the leopard will lie down with the goat, the calf and the lion and the yearling together; and a little child will lead them. The cow will feed with the bear, their young will lie down together, and the lion will eat straw like the ox.
The infant will play near the cobra's den, and the young child will put its hand into the viper's nest. They will neither harm nor destroy on all my holy mountain, for the earth will be filled with the knowledge of the Lord as the waters cover the sea.
- Isaiah 11:6-9

For here we have no lasting city, but we seek the city that is to come.
- Hebrews 13:14

How do you envision Heaven at this point? What parts of your description are most appealing to you? No more pain? Beautiful mansions? Joyful feasts? Seeing loved ones again? Resting your head on Jesus' chest in pure and perfect peace? Talking to the saints we've read about, like Moses, Paul or Mary? Make a list and examine why these are important to you.

Describe Heaven.

_____
_____
_____
_____
_____
_____
_____
_____
_____
_____

There will be a new you as well as a new Earth. Explore these passages.

But our citizenship is in Heaven, and from it we await a Savior, the Lord Jesus Christ, who will transform our lowly body to be like his glorious body, by the power that enables him even to subject all things to himself.
- Philippians 3:20-21

Just as we have borne the image of the man of dust, we shall also bear the image of the man of Heaven.
- 1 Corinthians 15:49

Behold! I tell you a mystery. We shall not all sleep, but we shall all be changed, in a moment, in the twinkling of an eye, at the last trumpet. For the trumpet will sound, and the dead will be raised imperishable, and we shall be changed.
- 1 Corinthians 15:51-52

He will wipe away every tear from their eyes, and death shall be no more, neither shall there be mourning, nor crying, nor pain anymore, for the former things have passed away.
- Revelation 21:4

So is it with the resurrection of the dead. What is sown is perishable; what is raised is imperishable. It is sown in dishonor; it is raised in glory. It is sown in weakness; it is raised in power. It is sown a natural body; it is raised a spiritual body. If there is a natural body, there is also a spiritual body.
- 1 Corinthians 15:42-44

What parts of your Earthy body/mind are you ready to be rid of and why? How do you think being a new you will feel? Does that bring you joy?

___
___
___
___
___
___
___
___
___
___
___
___

Yes, we are of good courage, and we would rather be away from the body and at home with the Lord. – 2 Corinthians 5:8

How does changing your earthly goals to a goal of Heaven affect you? Does it relieve worry and anxiety? Does it fill you with joy to know what awaits?

___

And not only the creation, but we ourselves, who have the first fruits of the Spirit, groan inwardly as we wait eagerly for adoption as sons, the redemption of our bodies. - Romans 8:23

Our human nature is to worry and be anxious about events we face.
Part of this final chapter in our Stone Story is learning to trust in God and not worry, to find joy always, even in the face of adversity. This may be the hardest step of all. Explore these verses:

Consider it pure joy, my brothers and sisters, whenever you face trials of many kinds, because you know that the testing of your faith produces perseverance. Let perseverance finish its work so that you may be mature and complete, not lacking anything.
- James 1:2-4

Trust in the Lord with all your heart; do not depend on your own understanding. Seek his will in all you do, and he will show you which path to take.
- Proverbs 3:5-6

Therefore, I tell you, do not worry about your life, what you will eat or drink; or about your body, what you will wear. Is not life more than food, and the body more than clothes? Look at the birds of the air; they do not sow or reap or store away in barns, and yet your heavenly Father feeds them. Are you not much more valuable than they? Can any one of you by worrying add a single hour to your life?
And why do you worry about clothes? See how the flowers of the field grow. They do not labor or spin. Yet I tell you that not even Solomon in all his splendor was dressed like one of these. If that is how God clothes the grass of the field, which is here today and tomorrow is thrown into the fire, will he not much more clothe you—you of little faith? So, do not worry,

saying, 'What shall we eat?' or 'What shall we drink?' or 'What shall we wear?' For the pagans run after all these things, and your heavenly Father knows that you need them. But seek first his kingdom and his righteousness, and all these things will be given to you as well. Therefore, do not worry about tomorrow, for tomorrow will worry about itself. Each day has enough trouble of its own.

- Matthew 6:25-34

We now have this light shining in our hearts, but we ourselves are like fragile clay jars containing this great treasure. This makes it clear that our great power is from God, not from ourselves.

We are pressed on every side by troubles, but we are not crushed. We are perplexed, but not driven to despair. We are hunted down, but never abandoned by God. We get knocked down, but we are not destroyed. Through suffering, our bodies continue to share in the death of Jesus so that the life of Jesus may also be seen in our bodies.

- 2 Corinthians 4:7-10

Have you been able to erase worry and anxiety from your life? How would your life change if you could remove them? Use the next pages to deeply examine the concept of life without worry or anxiety. Would you be more joyful? List examples.

_____

_____

_____

_____

_____

What steps can you take to increase your faith that God will carry you through adversity? Prayer? Study? Discussion with others? Counseling? Treatment of illness/mental illness? Are you willing to take these hard steps?

_____
_____
_____
_____
_____
_____
_____
_____
_____
_____
_____
_____
_____
_____
_____
_____
_____
_____
_____

"Worry never robs tomorrow of its sorrow, it only saps today of its joy."
- Leo F. Buscaglia

Do you feel guilty if you show happiness or joy in the face of personal adversity? Why? Societal norms? Upbringing? Fear of how you will be viewed by others? Desire for pity or attention? Be honest, look deep.

_____
_____
_____
_____
_____
_____
_____
_____
_____
_____
_____
_____
_____
_____
_____
_____
_____
_____
_____
_____
_____
_____
_____

"The mind is everything. What you think, you become." – Gautama Buddha

Can you change your underlying beliefs to allow you to feel happiness and joy in the face of adversity? What would you have to do?

_____
_____
_____
_____
_____
_____
_____
_____
_____
_____
_____
_____
_____
_____
_____
_____
_____
_____
_____

"Nothing can stop the man with the right mental attitude from achieving his goal; nothing on earth can help the man with the wrong mental attitude." – Thomas Jefferson

Is doubt an obstacle in your path?

If you find yourself in situations where you question why God has not answered your prayer. If you constantly question why a loving God would let terrible things like war and poverty and child abuse happen in this world…. I want you to stop. Stop for a minute and think of Jesus, God's precious son. Jesus knew he was about to endure one of the most horrible, painful deaths that can be imagined. He was going to have nails driven into his body and hang with his whole bodyweight dragging down on those nails. He wouldn't even be able to take in a soothing breath of cool air because the weight of his body had compressed his lungs to the point that there was little room for drawing in a breath. God also knew this was going to happen.

So even knowing the crucifixion was going to occur, it was still something Jesus desperately dreaded. So, He prayed to his Father. He prayed so hard to God to let him avoid being crucified, that his sweat became as great drops of blood.

If you have children, you know that you would do anything to keep them from being harmed. And if they came to you in tears and said, "Daddy or Mommy, please, don't let this thing hurt me." You would make sure that you didn't let it happen. Imagine how God felt in this situation.

God did let death claim His son, His beloved only son, and it proves his overwhelming, never ending love for us. And because Jesus and God are one, the pain and agony of that death was felt by God, as well. But he had to let it occur because it was part of his plan to save us.

Yes, God does answer prayers, but when He doesn't always answer the way you think he should, you have to assume that it's because there is a reason. And if you can learn to accept that, as hard as it may be, your faith deepens. The laser slices away a piece of your hard, outer shell.

Can you think of a time when God didn't answer a prayer the way you thought He should and it turned out okay over time? Were there lessons you learned from unanswered prayers that made you stronger, kinder, more patient, or humble? If you've never considered this, make a list of all the times you remember praying for something that didn't come to you in the way you prayed. Examine each situation in detail and determine if God answered your prayer another way or if there was a reason what you wanted wouldn't have been part of God's plan. There may be some events for which you can't yet determine this as it's yet to be revealed to you. That's okay. List them anyway and come back to them later when you see the path more clearly.

_____
_____
_____
_____
_____
_____
_____
_____
_____

The Jewel Stone.

Each time we choose joy over sadness, each time we trust God to provide when we have nothing, each time we put aside our doubts and just let him lead, those are like the precise cuts of a laser slicing off those last vestiges of flawed beliefs and thoughts.

When our faith is honed to perfection even from the smooth outer shell we developed in the river of life, then we find the perfect jewel inside. Just like when flawed pieces of a rough stone are cut away to reveal a stunning diamond that sends forth rainbows of beautiful light – we can become the polished and perfect soul that joins God, Jesus and all the saints in Heaven.

If you have not completed your Stone Story, you may not be ready to consider some of the concepts in this workbook. That's okay. Complete what you can and come back to it later when the process is more apparent and you're ready to accept the harder lessons and further transform.

Remember, it takes time for the rough river rock to become a smooth stone, so it may take you years to learn and change.

Currently, you might be in the rough stone stage, or the smooth stone stage, where your transformation is not as complete. You may still need some rough edges knocked off or some chunks of your smooth shell lasered away. You still have lessons to learn and wisdom to gain. In this stage it may be more difficult for you to accept the hardships of life. You could feel chastised by not feeling happiness in the face of adversity because you simply can't find the joy and you question God and have doubts. Your friends may nod knowingly and say you're having a "crisis of faith."

But those people who smugly nod may be wrong. The truth is, these hardships may actually be a period of growth and learning, allowing your faith to deepen. This is a complicated concept, but God does want you to live in joy. Even if we have times when our faith feels stretched to the limit. Even when we curse our doubts, knowing how it wounds God, even if we can't summon up even a thread of joy in the midst of tragedy, know that He still loves us and holds us close in his loving arms. He's going to wait for us to transform.

Think about this story from Genesis.
Adam and Eve eat of the tree that God forbade them to eat and realize they're naked. Out of shame, they make themselves clothes from leaves, a pretty pitiful type of clothing if you remember trying to knit leaves together with pine needles as a child. God finds them and basically lays serious curses on them for their disobedience. If you've read this passage you know that God is extremely angry with them. Their lack of faith in Him ruined every beautiful thing He had given them. But, He still cared for them, and listen to this example of his gentle kindness. - He sees their pathetic leaf clothes that are probably falling apart at that point, and surely not comfortable, and despite the fact that they have just served him the greatest of betrayals, he makes them clothes out of animal skins.

Think about how kind and forgiving He is to them after what they did. Do you think God loves you any less? Do you think your moments of doubt are in any way as hurtful as the unfaithful consequences of Adam and Eve disobeying Him?

So hopefully you can start thinking of this concept of hardships in life in a different way because it can lead to greater joy and deeper faith for you. Progress and feel the love of God and know that He is always there, patiently and tenderly waiting for you to find your way through your personal stone story, until you are finally revealed as the perfect jewel he will lovingly gather home.

Cut out a picture of a faceted polished jewel as you envision yourself becoming and tape it over the diamond shape below. Refer to this picture in times of doubt. Carry a smooth pebble in your pocket or purse to hold and feel when you need to recognize a hardship as a difficult moment of transition.

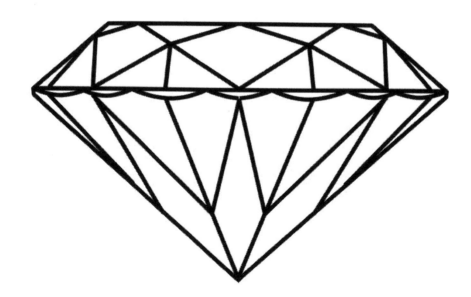

Use the rest of this book to Journal your Story of Stones. Go back and add to sections as revelations about events occur to you along the way. And remember:

For God so loved the world that he gave his one and only Son, that whoever believes in him shall not perish but have eternal life.
- John 3:16

_____
_____
_____
_____
_____
_____
_____
_____
_____
_____
_____
_____
_____
_____
_____
_____
_____
_____
_____